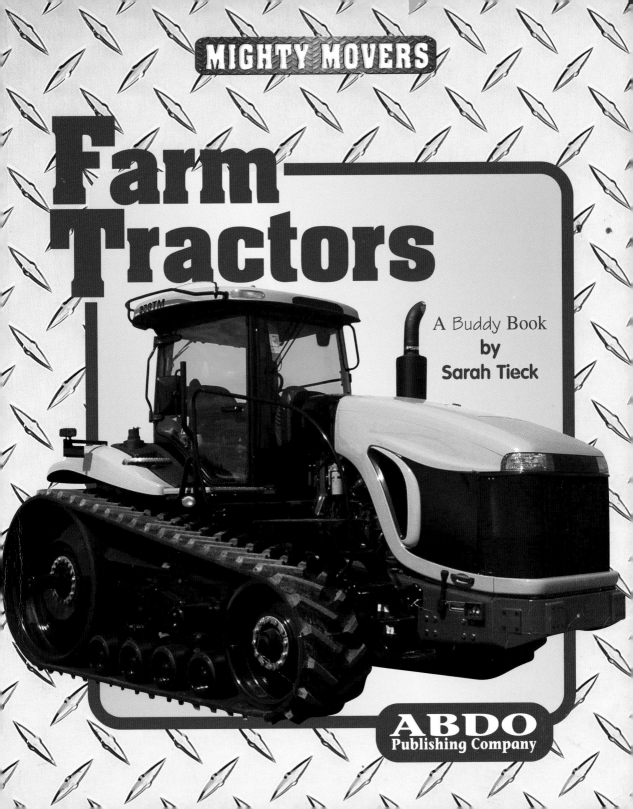

MIGHTY MOVERS

Farm Tractors

A Buddy Book
by
Sarah Tieck

ABDO
Publishing Company

VISIT US AT

www.abdopub.com

Published by ABDO Publishing Company, 4940 Viking Drive, Edina, Minnesota 55435.

Copyright © 2005 by Abdo Consulting Group, Inc. International copyrights reserved in all countries. No part of this book may be reproduced in any form without written permission from the publisher. Buddy Books™ is a trademark and logo of ABDO Publishing Company.

Printed in the United States.

Written and Edited by: Sarah Tieck
Contributing Editor: Michael P. Goecke
Graphic Design: Maria Hosley
Image Research: Sarah Tieck
Photographs: Maynard Agena, Corbis, Corel, Photodisc, Photos.com

Library of Congress Cataloging-in-Publication Data

Tieck, Sarah, 1976-
   Farm Tractors / Sarah Tieck.
       p. cm. — (Mighty movers)
   Includes index.
   ISBN 1-59197-827-0
       1. Farm tractors—Juvenile literature. I. Title

S711.T524 2005
629.225'2—dc22

2004050237

Table of Contents

What Is A Tractor?

A tractor is a farm machine. Farmers drive tractors. Tractors help farmers with farmwork.

Farmers use tractors to help put hay into bales.

PARTS OF A TRACTOR

Engine

Inside the Cab

Steps to enter the cab

Control Levers

Tractor Cab

Drawbar

Mud Guards

Tractor Tire

Power Take-off

What Do Tractors Do?

Tractors help with many jobs on a farm. Tractors pull other farming machines. These machines work with the tractor to do many jobs on a farm.

A tractor pulls a plow that breaks up dirt for planting. A tractor's trailer carries corn to the farm silo. A blade helps clean the barn.

A farmer plows the fields.

FARM TOOLS

Plow

Tractors pull plows. Plows help dig into dirt. Plows have sharp blades. Farmers use plows to get fields ready to plant crops.

Harrow

A tractor pulls a harrow. Harrows help get the dirt ready to plant. They make big lumps of dirt smaller.

Silo

A silo is a round building. Farmers use silos to hold chopped plants and grain.

How Tractors Work

Tractors have an engine like a car. They also have a steering wheel and headlights. The headlights help farmers drive the tractor at night.

Tractors have a hitch on the back. The hitch is called a drawbar. It connects the tractor to other farm machines. This helps the farmer do many jobs on the farm.

The drawbar helps connect other farm machines to the tractor.

Some tractors have a cab. The farmer sits in the cab. The cab's windows protect the farmer from dust.

A tractor's cab blocks out wind, dust, and rain.

Controls inside the cab help the farmer drive the tractor.

The tractor's controls are in the cab. The farmer moves levers. Levers make the tractor's tools move.

The parts of a tractor work because of something called hydraulics. Hydraulics is the use of liquids such as water and oil to move machines. Pressure created by the liquids makes the machine's parts move.

The other farming machines work because of something called the power take-off. The power take-off is like an engine. The power take-off helps machines hooked to the tractor work. The power take-off also helps drive machines pulled by the tractor.

A view of the power take-off.

How Tractors Move

Most tractors have tires. Some tractors have big tires. Some tractors have small tires. All tractor tires have a special shape. The tires have bumps. This shape helps tractors drive through rough fields.

Some tractors are called crawler tractors. Crawler tractors don't have tires. They move on tracks. The tracks let the crawler tractor move on soft land. They also help the tractor move on rough land.

Crawler tracks look and move differently than tires.

Changes In Farming

Before there were farm machines, people and horses did farmwork by hand. Farm machines made farmwork easier. Farm machines also helped people grow more food.

The first farm tractors changed farming. Tractors made work easier for farmers. Tractors also made farmwork faster. Farmers could grow more food for more people.

In 1914, many men left their farms to fight in World War I. People and soldiers needed food. It was hard to grow enough food. There were not enough people to help. Tractors helped families do the farmwork while the farmers were away.

Horses helped with farmwork.

Tractors Today

There are many kinds of tractors. Some are old and some are new. Tractors still help farmers with farmwork. Tractors are the reason farmers can grow enough food to feed many people.

Tractors help farmers harvest crops.

Not all tractors are used for work. Some people collect old tractors. Old tractors are called antiques. Antiques are found in museums and at shows.

There are many kinds of antique tractors.

Important Words

antique something that was made a long time ago.

blade a metal tool that hooks on to a tractor. The blade works like a shovel to push dirt.

engine a machine that creates energy to make something run or move.

hydraulics the force of liquids, used to make machines move.

lever a bar that an operator moves to make a machine move.

plow a farming tool that cuts into soil. Tractors pull plows.

silo a round building that farmers use for storing corn and grain.

trailer a wagon that is pulled by a tractor.

Web Sites

To learn more about farm tractors, visit ABDO Publishing Company on the World Wide Web. Web site links about farm tractors are featured on our Book Links page. These links are routinely monitored and updated to provide the most current information available.

www.abdopub.com

Index